PEE WHERE YOU WANT

Man's Best Friend
Talks
Back!

Unleashed
Edition

KAREN H. THOMPSON

THE DOTTIN PUBLISHING GROUP 🔥 FRANKLIN, TN

PEE WHERE YOU WANT
The Dottin Publishing Group
P.O. Box 682701
Franklin, TN 37068-2701
www.peewhereyouwant.com

Edited by Alice Sullivan
Book design by TLC Graphics, *www.TLCGraphics.com*
Cover: Monica Thomas, Interior: Erin Stark
Beagle cover photo: istockphoto.com © Ryan Lane
Author photo by: Nora Canfield

ISBN: 978-0-9847853-0-8

Printed in the United States of America

To my dog Max, thanks for adopting me!

MAX
1994 – 2010

CONTENTS

SELF-ESTEEM

PARENTING

INTRODUCTION

Anyone who thinks dogs are stupid has clearly never owned one. Just watch an owner with their dog for a few minutes and you'll see that man's best friend has got their owner wrapped around their paw. After all, dogs, more so than any other animal, have mastered the art of manipulation to the point where humans are carrying them around in designer bags with monogrammed sweaters and bottled water. Who's the dumb one, you say? I don't see dogs paying $2 for bottled water when there's perfectly good free water available in the toilet.

Pee Where You Want is a compilation of wisdom from my brilliant dog, Max. After 15 wonderful years together, Max passed away, but not before he taught me his most important lesson. He taught me how to stop whining and start living my life *for me*. During his final days, he showed me how to go all out for my dreams, regardless of what anybody else thought.

Even though he couldn't hear as well as he once did and he often bumped into walls, Max still managed to stroll with a swagger. He peed where and when he wanted. He didn't want anyone's pity and he lived a full life. Max was a mix of so many different breeds I couldn't even tell you what he was other than loyal, loving, confident, and too damn funny for words. Max

taught me to lighten up, speak my mind, and stop caring so much about what other people thought.

Max poured all of his wisdom into *Pee Where You Want*. In his words: "We're sick and tired of listening to you humans whine about how hard you work, why your boyfriend left you, or why your butt didn't get a promotion." Hey, big baby, news-flash—snap out of it! Man up and take charge of your life! Better yet, let "man's best friend" show you how to *live a life unleashed*.

LIFESTYLE
and
RELATIONSHIPS

KEEPER • CHASKA, MN

CHAPTER ONE

WORK LIKE A DOG

Okay, this whole "retirement" thing that you people go on about, like it's the Holy Grail moment of your life, just baffles the hell out of us dogs. I mean, you say that you've spent the last forty-plus years of your life "working like a dog" to then retire. Really? Hmmm, let's examine the whole "work like a dog" statement.

What do you people actually think we dogs do all day? Huh? I'll tell you this, we don't put on tight uncomfortable clothes that make us conform to some standard, spend hours in close quarters with people that we otherwise wouldn't even want to have a drink with (let alone meet with), and work side-by-side with for 8–10 hours a day, five days a week. And then, if that's not enough, you supposedly highest being on the food chain, exchange emails and texts with those people for another few hours every night, early in the morning, *and* on weekends. Some of you really "successful" people even keep this going while you're on vacation or attending your kid's events...you know, during your "down time."

Now let's look at what we dogs consider "working like a dog." Our typical day begins with a nice long stretch before we wake up our still-sleeping owners to go to the bathroom and for a walk to get our morning exercise. Ah, there's nothing like a little stroll in the fresh morning air and chasing a few squirrels as we stop to smell *every* bush. We would prefer to get an hour or so of a morning workout but no, our owners have to hit the gym or the office early. So, off we go, back home to be served breakfast with a nice refreshing bowl of water that we slowly savor.

Some days we even get a few extra minutes of a light rub with an inspirational talk reminding us how special we are to our owners. Then a quick "I love you" as our owner grabs an energy bar and rushes out the door. With tummies full and our first of two workouts done, we sleep for several hours, changing positions and rooms as we check out various noises.

Thank God for our favorite tech gadget, the security system. What a lifesaver. Now, we dogs just have to wait for the alarm signal before we decide to check out the noise that disrupted our naptime. Ah, gotta love the technology that you humans worked so hard developing.

We put in a solid 8 or more hours a day, five consecutive days of active resting, to prepare for the countless hours of counseling we do every evening when our blessed owner returns home. That's right, it takes a lot of preparation to act interested in your days which, to be honest, are not always so interesting. That, my friend, is "working like a dog."

MAX'S TRAINING TIPS
for HUMANS

TIP #1   **Find a sugar daddy,** sugar momma, or both—whatever your preference. There's no judgment here so "do you." The goal here is to find someone to finance the lifestyle that you should be accustomed to living.

TIP #2   **Find some free** and seemingly sincere people who will listen to your incessant complaining about trivial crap. The key here is for these people to always gaze into your eyes as if you are brilliant and totally misunderstood by society. This one will be challenging to maintain for many years so be prepared to add this maintenance expense to your sugar daddy's/momma's/combo credit card.

TIP #3   **This one is crucial** to successfully applying the first two tips, so pay close attention. Workout every day to maintain some level of fitness. You are going to have to be viewed as attractive by your chosen sugar daddy/momma so keeping up your appearance to meet their needs is critical. Competition is tight for a good sugar daddy/momma position, so you better be prepared to do anything necessary to maintain your role. That's right, your opinion of what's attractive doesn't matter. As a matter of fact, most of your opinions don't really matter at all. Your opinions should be aligned solely with your money source. Got a problem with that? Then go back to working for your damn self but let's be clear, if you want to "work like a dog" then immediately put my training tips into practice.

CUSTOMER SERVICE can REVIVE your ECONOMY

You know it amazes me that you people complain about "those damn illegal immigrants taking jobs away from hard-working citizens." Really, hard-working citizens? Hmm, have you paid attention to some of those "so-called hard workers" lately? Well I observed some of your "hard workers" recently while out with my owner and let me tell you, parakeets have more personality than some of you humans!

I nearly passed out waiting for the walking dead at the fast food restaurant to get my owner's order right. First of all, Mumbles, open your friggin' mouth and actually speak English. Say it with me: "Hello, may I help you?" And not "Huh, what you want?"

Listen, I'm not fluent in ignorant dumbass but aren't you supposed to actually smile while you're giving a customer feedback on how they look in an outfit that you're trying to sell, as opposed to rolling your eyes and saying, "it's alright." Here's a tip, let's actually act like we want to get paid for working. I know it's a crazy thought but maybe if we stopped focusing on someone else "stealing your job" and started to actually work hard, deliver quality service, and show up on time—even on Fridays and Mondays—then maybe we wouldn't have to worry about employers hiring undocumented workers or outsourcing your jobs to another country. *I'm just saying.*

WORK-LIFE BALANCE AIN'T WHAT IT USED TO BE

For at least the last century, you humans have traded places with dogs. Ah, advancement. Traditionally, man's best friend worked alongside him toiling in the fields, herding sheep, hunting, and protecting the other animals. You even made us stay outside at night to watch your home. That's right. Dogs never got a chance to sleep. And, what did we get in exchange for this life of slavery? Table scraps that couldn't satisfy a cat! Don't even get me started on what would happen if a fox got into the chicken coop and one of your beloved chickens got taken. Oh yeah, everyone was quick to say, "Let's kill the dog." Why? Just because we didn't want to risk our life for a *damn chicken*. Whatever!

Anyway, over the decades as civilization advanced, you humans found a way to automate most of our work. Again, we gotta love your creativity! We went from spending nearly 95 percent of our time working to now spending about 5 percent, on average, of our time working. We did all of this without complaining "man, we work too hard," "we need a union to fight for better work conditions," or (we dogs really love this one) "we need work-life balance programs to help us be more productive." What the hell is all of this soft, whiny crap? Are you friggin' kidding me? I just want to pee all over your damn human resource policies.

Hey, top of the food chain, how about you stop your damn whining and…I don't know, do something novel like stop trying to "have it all." That's right. I said it. You want the big house, exotic vacations, and oh, don't forget Princess's over-the-top, totally unnecessary "Sweet Sixteen" party.

You work non-stop; about 90 percent of your time is spent slaving away to live the dream, to keep up with the Joneses. All of this while you complain incessantly about how hard you work. If I have to hear one more person in the dog park bragging (which, by the way, sounds just like a whiny cat) about how many hours he put in working, I'm going to pee all over his legs.

You want work-life balance? Start focusing on getting "LIFE-PLAY-WORK balance." "Work-life balance" just perpetuates the myth that you can have it all. Wrong, wrong, wrong! Just by switching your stupid term to "life-play-work" balance should help you people with your human resource gurus, consultants, and unions, figure out how to get the same income and productivity while creating more time to enjoy the fruits of your labor. Think about it, people.

MAX'S TRAINING TIPS
for HUMANS

TIP #1   Let's redefine what it means to "have it all" in this new world of life-play-work balance. First of all, we are going to restructure your work schedules to no more than 50 hours a week, on average. That's right, simmer down you over achievers, you won't lose your jobs. Now during work hours, you're actually going to do something novel, your jobs, that's all. Those additional 10–20 hours are going to shift to your play activities. After all, you were already spending that time during the day managing your online virtual friendships, losing money on your fantasy sports teams, and solving the world's problems with your co-worker Bob who's bound to get fired one of these days. So with your remaining time, you can start enjoying your life while you're still healthy enough to walk your loyal dog. I'll get my leash.

TIP #2   You need to stop trying to keep up with the Joneses and start keeping up with the Chen's. Have you taken a look at the global financial reports lately? Notice anything different? The American and European markets are struggling to rebound from their debt while the Asian markets are growing. Oh yeah, and I just heard that Japan is one of the biggest lenders to other countries. Hmm, do you feel that shift? Let's wake up people and live within your budgets.

MUTT RULE:
UNIONS NEED an EXTREME MAKEOVER

Dogs really do understand why you people originally created unions to protect the rights of the average Joe from corporations, many of whom would treat them like modern-day slaves, if they could get away with it legally. However, times have changed, people, and we need to reinvent unions to fight for things that really matter. I get that union members want to continue receiving healthcare benefits at below average premiums but what if the company is losing money and they ship your jobs overseas? What did we really win? And is your teacher's union really winning a major victory when all teachers get to keep their jobs in when their students are failing miserably? Is that still winning?

Let's get "extreme" and have unions negotiate for benefits that are in line with market rates and institute incentives for their union members to improve their health. Let's also get radical and implement contract terms where members are required to meet minimum performance standards that will be established by an oversight coalition of members, employers, lawyers, citizens, and customers.

If you can't perform then you're fired. Hmm, accountability is a beautiful thing. Now that's a makeover!

CHAPTER THREE

NORMAN ROCKWELL IS DEAD

Remember the good ole days when you looked forward to calling someone on the phone to hear what was going on in his or her life?

I remember my owner would talk on the phone for hours, laughing about the latest gossip. This would give me plenty of time to sneak into the trashcan for a quick bite or roll around in the laundry pile. Yep, those were the good ole days.

Oh, and remember those great family dinners you used to have when I would sit underneath the table, getting scraps of food from the kids, while the parents talked about their day at work and the kids told them how things were going in school? Yeah, those were the good times.

These days I'm lucky to even get a scrap of food from a fast-food container while I watch my family text, update their Facebook statuses, and read what their online twitter community is doing! All of this while they barely say one word to each other. Hmmm, quality family time? I think you people are missing the point of all of this damn technology. It's supposed to make life easier, not separate families.

I mean, things are really getting bad when I can't even count on my owners to send their kids to their room as punishment. This used to mean that I would get the kid's undivided attention as they told me how mean and stupid you parents were to them. We would make plans to escape, which I always thought was stupid since neither one of us had any money, which even dogs know is necessary to make it in the world. But I didn't mind because I was getting rubbed so, talk on baby!

Now with all of your advanced technology, punishment sucks because the little brat has a flat screen TV, laptop, and cell phone which, you guessed it, means that they don't have a free hand to rub my belly. That's just wrong! Hello, punishment should *hurt*!

With all of these gadgets, how in the hell can these kids come up with their heart-felt apology so that they can rejoin their loving family and watch television together? Oh wait, that would interfere with expanding your online community and selling your virtual produce to your virtual friends. This just may be why you parents don't know that your little bundle of joy is planning an attack on his classmates, or worse yet, plotting a cyber attack on a foreign government with his so-called harmless little online social community!

MAX'S TRAINING TIPS
for HUMANS

TIP #1 Run—don't walk—into your kid's bedroom and remove everything but their bed, clothes, and toiletries. That's right; strip it down to the bare minimum. Don't worry about how they feel, damn it, this isn't a democracy, it's a friggin' dictatorship and the little darlings should be happy to have a roof over their heads, clothes on their back, and a meal on the table.

TIP #2 Now let's put all of the gadgets that we took back from junior's room and put them to some really good use in a space where they can really be appreciated; a room that will provide you with years of happiness: our new "Parents Only" room. Well, parents and dogs only room. After all, your sanctuary wouldn't be the same without "man's best friend" by your side. Oh yeah, as an extra precaution, let's get a comfy dog bed that will match your decorating motif, so that I can keep guard by the door to keep the kids out of your retreat. Now, this will be the *new* good ole days!

MUTT RULE:
A NAME means EVERYTHING

Pay close attention here, we are supposedly your best friend. If you don't want to set us up for a lifetime of abuse by other dogs and your damn judgmental friends, then please think before naming us. We don't do cutesy, soft, or ghetto-fabulous names that nobody can pronounce. So, if I get beat down in the park or doggie daycare because your dumb behind gave me a "special" name, I'm gonna bite your ass the next time you think we're just playing around. Go fetch is going to have a little extra twist.

I'm just saying...think carefully before picking your dog's name.

CHAPTER FOUR

FOLLOWERS, FANS, FRIENDS, OR IDIOTS

"Hey, I just pooped on my owners couch!"

"OMG, I can't believe it's MONDAY already, back to the grind of doggie daycare...ugh."

Hmmm, sounds pathetic, even boring, right? Remember when your mother taught you not to be a follower, to have your own opinions, and to choose your friends wisely? All great advice that you fools have somehow ignored in your quest to have thousands of complete strangers, random acquaintances, or long-forgotten so-called friends become your intimate confidants. What the hell? We don't have these people over to the house for a reason...we don't really like them.

I know that all of you either have some form of ADD or are just too busy to actually engage in deep meaningful conversations that go beyond 140 characters, but this virtual online world is getting a little out of hand. Seriously, don't you think it's a bit odd to spend several hours online, each day, telling "friends/followers/fans" the intimate details of your life, as if those people really cared? Get over yourself!

Think about it, since when did it become interesting to complain about your job to everyone you've ever known? Or better yet, tell the world that you had an amazing night with your mate. Whatever!

MAX'S TRAINING TIPS for HUMANS

TIP #1 Next time you want to post your life status for the tenth time in a day, STOP, get your dog's leash, and go for a walk. While walking—here comes the tough part—put your phone on silent and put it away.

Stay with me now, look around as you walk and actually speak to one of the random strangers walking by you. What, you don't talk to strangers? Ah, you do every day online to people that you'll never meet. So, get over your social deficiencies and just say, "Hi, great day huh?" Sound lame? Oh yeah, like "I just fed my imaginary pig in Farmville, won't you join me?" isn't the most dumb ass thing you've ever heard. Take a chance, open your mouth, and let it flow.

TIP #2 **Just like your therapist confirmed,** your mother is crazy, but she did give you at least one piece of solid advice: Don't follow the crowd. "If everyone jumped off the bridge, would you?" Yep, remember that dumb question? This was, and still is, a rhetorical question, so stop signing up to follow complete strangers on Twitter. It's sad to watch you all spend hours texting away on your latest mobile device. Especially while you're with another person, who just so happens to be texting someone else. Yeah, that's quality time. I can't imagine why you people keep getting divorced.

TIP #3 **Apply this new rule of thumb** before building your online empire of friends/fans/followers. If you wouldn't have a drink with this person, then DON'T issue or accept an online request to be a friend/fan/follower.

I know, God forbid you only have a few hundred people on your list. Oh yeah, others in your online world will judge you harshly for having so few people, but what does it matter? Since when do we care what Bob from the 10th grade (who, by the way, never had a date with anyone who wasn't his cousin) thinks about you? After all, Bob just lost his job, AGAIN, so he's back living at home with his parents. Sure, his opinion should really matter. Wake up and get a damn life!

MUTT RULE:
SEXT TODAY, PAY TOMORROW

I can't believe that I even have to give you this rule. Never, ever put anything in writing that could come back to haunt you. Let's say when you're running for political office and you're sexting with your lover, who's coincidentally NOT your spouse, about the steamy night you have planned for them. What the hell are you humans doing with your so-called advanced technology? Damn, even a Chihuahua knows not to send a picture of their private parts with some lame caption "daddy can't wait to share his nuts with you" to somebody knowing damn well that some day, when you piss that person off, they will now have the perfect ammunition to use against you.

Oh yeah, don't be surprised that the skank who quickly sent you that sexy text is now on television standing beside her self-righteous lawyer claiming how hurt she was to find out that you were married and that you lied to her. Yeah right, it's amazing how fast skanks get smart enough to hire a high-priced lawyer and agent just minutes after you tell her it's over.

Hmmm, it's a good thing you called her over twenty times when you were drunk to tell her how much you hated her and that you would ruin her career at the strip club, oops, I mean her acting and modeling career. But hey, look on the bright side. Just remember that no one really gets their whole 15 minutes of fame anymore; it's more like 8 minutes, so cheer up, you big freak.

CHAPTER FIVE

PLAYING THE FIELD, DOGGY STYLE

There's nothing sadder than watching you humans on a date. Oh wait, there is something worse...listening to you complain about how much you hate dating. Why you all have so much trouble finding a mate, or better yet, why you put so much energy into the search cracks us dogs up. You should hear the stories we tell in the park. Man, there are some good ones!

We dogs keep it simple. When you see a dog with a nice tail, you run over to get a closer look before the rest of the pack notices. You come up from behind to get a nice long sniff of the booty. I tell you, if the smell isn't right then you can stop right there. If that checks out, then you make your way around to the face just to make sure things still look good up close. There's nothing worse than a nice booty with an ugly face.

Now, onto the personality. If they stand around and let you check them out without biting you or trying to fight you then, oh boy, have you found your match. Yep, it's just that simple.

Within 5 minutes of seeing, sniffing, and a brief little rub of the noses, our relationship is underway!

MAX'S TRAINING TIPS
for HUMANS

TIP #1 forget all of that crazy mess about conducting background checks or spying on a prospective mate to see what you might be getting yourself into before things get too serious. Let's keep it simple and go old-school here, people.

First, Google them to make sure that you've caught all of the obvious stuff. You know, things like were they a former convict, dead-beat parent, or still married. Once, you've crossed these issues off your "dating checklist," next we employ a very simple but fail-proof test that dogs have used since the beginning of time. The sniff test! What, you've never heard of this test? No wonder your relationships are so screwed up.

Once you see someone you like, just take a quick sniff test before you commit. That's right, get a good sniff while you're getting cozy. Don't worry if they catch you. Just play it off with a seemingly sincere compliment. Now, if you're not quick on your feet (okay, a polished liar), then rehearse this trick before-hand with a friend. Just say something like "wow, what's that cologne you're wearing?" Now, stay cool and maintain that fake "I'm interested in you" look even if your nose hairs are burned by the funk that you just inhaled. Slowly lean back while you smile slightly and say, "Hmm, that's interesting. I don't think

I've ever smelled a scent quite like that one." Okay, this isn't actually a lie since you probably haven't smelled anything this bad and this close up that wasn't wrapped up in a trash bag. Just keep smiling as you think of a way to end this date. And eventually, this relationship.

That's right. If the booty and the rest of the body don't smell right, then let it go! As a matter of fact, if it smells, just get up and walk away without saying anything. All manners are gone when the booty stinks.

TIP #2   **Love means never having** to spend time with your partner's family, friends, or co-workers when they're idiots. That's right, just because you fell in love with your "sweetie" doesn't mean that you have to spend time with these other people. Okay, well maybe we'll make an exception for the family members but only on special occasions. Other than those days, you don't have to see the crazy uncle or the cousin that everyone questions if they were secretly adopted or the product of a bad one-night stand. But, all of the other jerks don't get a pass on this tip. Let's keep it moving and focus on the only relationship that matters and it doesn't include these outsiders!

SKIP the DOG CRATE and GET a DOG WALKER

It takes us dogs awhile to be fully house trained. And yes, there are moments when we can't hold it until you get home. I know, we should *know how* to hold it for 8 friggin' hours while you're working, but things happen, man. Why don't you hold it all day and see how you feel?

So, when we do pee on your precious carpet, don't rub our face in it to teach us a lesson. Newsflash, we know it's our pee and we'll do it again if you don't cough up the cash to hire us a dog walker! Yeah, that's right, I said it.

How about this: if we don't get a mid-day walk, then the next time super stud misses the bowl, we're going to knock you down and rub *your* nose in it.

CHAPTER SIX

PIMP THAT ATHLETE

One of the greatest mysteries with you people is how in the hell some of your talented athletes can throw away their careers after only a few short years, over some really dumbass things. Have you looked at some of these athletes lately? Not many of them could find another job where they could legally earn millions of dollars in their 20s, not with their skill set. I'm not being mean but come on, I don't know of one company who would pay a barely literate, but often charismatic, twenty-something a multi-million dollar salary. And you don't either, so listen up college athletes, we're going to need you to follow just a few simple rules that will hopefully lengthen your careers.

First, refrain from allegedly committing crimes until *after* your professional career is over. That would really help everybody out. And by everybody, I mean the college athletic departments, professional leagues, and sports agents.

We get that you're a product of your environment and this whole college setting may be new to you but last time I checked, millions of dogs are rescued from the streets every year and brought into loving homes. You never see us shelter dogs jump on someone in the dog park and threaten them until they turn over their food, just because we were forced to rummage through garbage cans to survive while we were on the mean streets. Nope, not us.

So tell me why in the hell do you steroid taking, thuggish, pampered athletes expect everyone to look the other way when you break the rules? Seriously, it wouldn't hurt your dumb behinds to stay out of trouble, limit the number of your collegiate groupies, and focus on your short-lived sports career for a few years.

Finally, will you please learn to read so that you can understand the damn multi-million dollar contract that you'll hopefully sign, if you can keep things together. Oh yeah, while you're at it, how about keeping your parents out of the media and away from agents until after we actually know your behind will make it to the pros.

So go ahead, practice your victory dance and what you'll say during the post-game interviews, because Lord knows you mumbling, budding role models will need all of the practice you can get.

Don't forget to give your loyal dog a shout out when you make it to the big leagues!

MAX'S TRAINING TIPS
for HUMANS

TIP #1 Since you're the pride and joy of your family, neighborhood, and numerous other wanna be "friends," how about your loving parents get one of your reliable side-kicks, let's say Pookie (there's always someone in the entourage with that nickname), to keep you OUT of trouble and out of the media spotlight for a few years.

Now I know this may sound stupid but just stay with me for a minute. It's in Pookie's best interest to make sure that his meal ticket makes it to the pros and plays for at least a few seasons to secure some endorsements and the contract bonus money. Think about it, if the athlete can say have only two kids by one baby momma, thus reducing the number of court cases requiring hefty child support and hush money to keep the groupie quiet, while she lives the lifestyle that she has somehow gotten accustomed to so quickly, then that's more money for you and Pookie to split. See, you're starting to see the doggie wisdom.

TIP #2 Now, if we're all going to milk the life out of this athlete, then we're going to have think about building a global brand.

First, you're going to need to come up with a stupid ghetto saying to stand out from the other athletes. It's not like it used to be when athletes were admired for just their on-field abilities. No, now if they are going to have a successful career and be held up to incredibly high standards that society will eventually use to tear them apart, we're going to have to be creative.

Maybe we could get a reality show letting the world into some aspect of their life. Oh no, all of the really trashy ghetto fabulous themes have already been taken.

I got it—let's design a new-age multi-media, viral branding campaign about the people in the athlete's inner circle. Yeah, that's never been done before. I can see it now. A mobile app showing you how to become a baby momma or a video game teaching you how to identify an athlete in the making and secure your spot as his "Pookie." That's right! You, too, can become the next millionaire Pookie! I can see the money rolling in now.

🐾 MUTT RULE:
PLAN EARLY or PAY LATER... a VISION will SAVE YOU MONEY and your RETIREMENT

This one should be self-explanatory but let me quickly break it down for you people. As a family unit we need to pull together to create a realistic game plan for our kid's lives. After that first moment when you look into your children's beautiful eyes, right before they leave you sleep deprived and kill your sex life, let's get to planning their bright future of self sufficiency. The goal here with this early planning approach is to establish a blueprint for the kids' success to ensure that they leave home immediately after high school.

I know what you're saying, "It's too early to make this kind of plan. I want my kids to make their own choices about their career. I'm not a dictator." Stop the madness, people, and think about your own futures, and your loyal dogs, too. Your house should be run like a dictatorship. After all, do any of these kids bring money into the household? Nope. Do they cook, clean, or maintain the house? Again, nope. So tell me why we should give them a say about how long they drain your wallets?

I think you may be starting to see my point of view on this one. Stay with me now. All you have to do at this early stage is decide which path you want your kids to pursue. Option A: live off of their parents until they find their calling sometime in their mid-twenties, if you're lucky, or Option B: train the little darlings to become independent business owners who will legally contribute to our economy and perhaps even give you a job after your company ships your job overseas. Do I hear any votes for Option B? This is a win-win for everybody.

If the kid can walk, then they can work. It can begin really easy. Maybe you could make little scented sleeping masks for your little moneymaker to sell to their pre-school classmates to use during nap time. Cha ching! This is Option B thinking at its finest. Start early so that we can cruise our way to retirement. All aboard the Option B train!

POLITICS

CEDAR • BOISE, ID

CHAPTER SEVEN

DOG PARK POLITICS

Unlike your offices, there are very little politics in the dog park. That's right, we dogs like to keep things simple. We don't spend our time whining or saying things like: "I didn't get invited to Skippy's party" like you humans do. Why, you ask? Because we just don't *care*! Sure it may slight us for a couple of seconds when we see all of the dogs huddled together in the park suddenly split up when the uninvited dog trots on over. But hey, in a few minutes when we see someone go by on a motorcycle, all of that self-pity is forgotten as we start chasing the motorcycle together.

See, there's no room in the dog world for all of that soft, touchy feely crap, and no other dog from the group is going to trot over to see how we're feeling or to tell us that the party really wasn't that good anyway. Why? Because it's just not that important! Watch and learn, people. We dogs can be in heaven just by rolling in the grass, chasing a biker, and sniffing some balls. It just doesn't take that much to maintain the peace in the dog park.

MAX'S TRAINING TIPS
for HUMANS

TIP #1 What do you do when your weasel of a co-worker takes credit for the presentation that you stayed up all night to finish, when the jerk only stepped in at the last minute to fix a few typos? After your presentation is over, casually walk straight up to the "suck-up," look him straight in the eye, growl, and punch him dead in his throat. Now if you hit him just right, you'll knock the wind out of him and he'll gasp for air while looking at you with shock. Here's the real trick, you just walk away real slow without saying a word but you look back one more time and give him a glare to let him know that you're just crazy enough to come back and beat the living crap out of him if he ever takes credit for your work again. Situation resolved.

TIP #2 You find out that your co-worker is sleeping with your boss. Naturally, you're disgusted (a dog wouldn't be, but I'm trying to put myself in your shoes) but you recognize that this little situation presents you with a great opportunity to get assigned to that new project that you've had your eye on for awhile.

So, as you're casually talking with the office ho about her weekend, which, by the way, you already know includes a hookup with the married boss, just mention, "Hey, you know, it would be great if you recommended me to join that new project team. Don't you think?" Now the ho will try to get snippy with you and act like she can't help you. This is when you get a little closer to her and use the glare that you perfected in Tip #1 to ask her one more time to help you out because you'd hate to post something on her Facebook wall about this office fling but hey, it could happen if you slip and forget. All of a sudden, the ho will change her tune and next thing you know, you're heading up that new project. Ah, the power of persuasion.

TIP #3 When you finally get that great new job and you start planning how you're going to hand in your resignation, remember to exit with grace. As you shake your boss's hand and thank him for the experience, stand tall, embrace your inner dog, and pee on your boss's leg. Make sure that you cap this little trick off with a "you can kiss my ass" as you turn to walk out the door. Now, be careful, this may get you escorted out of the building by security, but what the hell, it was worth it.

I realize that this trick can really only be done by the alpha males, sorry ladies. But you can still do the "kiss my ass" comment as you leave and don't be disappointed, you, too, will probably get a security escort. You're embracing you inner alpha dog so YOU DON'T CARE!

MUTT RULE:
PETS in the OFFICE...
STOP the MADNESS

What the hell are you humans thinking? Oh right, "this will be great for all of us." Isn't that what you also told the American Indians? And look how that worked out for them, banished to some God-forsaken reservation. Have you been to a reservation lately? Yeah right, that's what I thought. Ah, no thanks. I'll pass on this offer. This isn't progress, it's bull.

We spend enough time together already and we really don't want to meet the brown-nosers that you complain about all of the time. And stop saying, "having my dog at work would make me more productive and happier." Liar! Man up and do your damn job without us. No dogs in the workplace!

CHAPTER EIGHT

CONSERVATIVES, LIBERALS, AND TV PUNDITS:

THE ULTIMATE CAGE MATCH FIGHT

Are you people friggin' kidding me? What the hell are you arguing about? Liberals, Conservatives, Christian Coalition, Tea Party Movement, Libertarians...can't you people all just get along? If mutts and pedigrees can co-exist in the dog park, then why can't you politicians work things out?

I know I'm just a dog, but from where I sit, you all pretty much sound the same. Every four years or so, we sit back and watch each of your political parties tear the other one apart; then someone has the nerve to question the patriotism of the other party just because they belong to an opposing party. Then, some loud mouth will go on TV to whine about how poorly their candidate was treated. What the hell? You mean to tell me that you can't find one issue to agree upon? Really?

All I'm saying is that maybe, if you all just took off those uptight suits, went to the park, caught a few Frisbees, sniffed a few balls, and rolled in some crap instead of talking so much crap then maybe you'd be able to sit around the table together and get some damn work done for a change.

MAX'S TRAINING TIPS
for HUMANS

TIP #1 The next time one of your fellow congressmen gets caught up in partisan posturing and stands up in the hallowed halls of congress, let's say in the middle of a televised presidential speech, to yell out "liar," here's what you do. Quietly get up and come up behind the deviant, grab them by the back of their neck while you whisper in their ear "shut the hell up, get out of your chair *now*, and walk with me." Now, the deviant may be tempted to shout out something else but place your other hand around his mouth.

By this point, the rest of your pack, I mean, a few of your close colleagues, will meet you in the aisle to "escort" the jackass out to the hallway. This is when the real human trick kicks in.

While one of your colleagues blocks the door, the others should form a circle so that you can whoop his behind like the junkyard dog that he apparently wants to be. Don't worry about the media taking pictures because if the cameraman gets ready to film this scene you just growl, show your teeth, and send one member of your pack to persuade them that it would be advantageous to lose his film and go take a coffee break, NOW!

TIP #2 *Schedule weekly play dates* with members of the opposing political parties. That's right, mix it up with some members of the liberal elite media, conservative angry media, disgruntled radio hosts, and those free-wheeling online journalists. Now, it will get funky in the beginning until you break the ice with the first "accidental" bump that will inevitably turn into a short-lived fight. Don't worry, this is necessary to level out the playing field and remind everyone that what happens on the playground, stays on the playground.

Also, to keep the dynamics balanced and to keep things interesting don't forget to include an even number of members from each of the groups. Oh yeah, no cameras or cell phones allowed. There's nothing like taking in the fresh air while you roll in the grass and chase balls to bond a pack and forget about your differences. Maybe then your leaders could pass a damn bill or two so we could get this country back on track!

MUTT RULE:
EVERYONE'S OPINION doesn't COUNT

Now I know what happened to some of those brown-nosers and geeks from high school that my damn owner brought to the house when I was a puppy…they grew up to be TV commentators! With flashbacks of not having a date to their high school prom or hanging out with their other band members on a Saturday night watching TV in the basement, these so-called experts are just pissed off at the world and hell-bent on showing everyone who ignored them in high school how they can destroy someone else's career.

Wow, it must feel great to get paid to pick someone else apart and tell the world what you would have done better to solve the country's problems. Yea, that would be impressive if these gurus of nothing actually spent any time in their lives doing even one of the jobs that they now get paid to rip apart publicly. Go back to your basements!

CHAPTER NINE

MUTTS VS. PEDIGREES
CAN'T WE ALL JUST GET ALONG?

We dogs will never understand why you humans discriminate against one another. This whole religious hatred thing kind of sounds like it should go against your so-called belief system, that is, unless you worship the devil. That's just weird. No seriously, we can't figure you people out on this issue. You all look alike to us dogs anyway. Really, we can't tell a country boy from the south apart from a fast talking northerner.

You'd never see dogs shun Skip and Steve just because they only like to "play" with the other male dogs. Also, a pedigree with a dog walker and designer vest would never get beaten up in the dog park because of how it was dressed. We know it was his damn owner's fault anyway.

Now, don't get me wrong, dogs will shun one another but it's for something more important like for being too friendly with cats or fighting with all the dogs just because you're mad that you got fixed before you even got a chance to use your equipment. Or worse yet, for smelling like humans, with that awful cologne.

Man up, roll in some crap, and get dirty. Now say it with me, "I'm funky and I'm proud." Ah funk, it's the true equalizer.

MAX'S TRAINING TIPS
for HUMANS

TIP #1 The only tip I can give you here (and I think it's my best one yet) is to cut the shit and get over yourself! If you don't like someone because they're different, just shut the hell up about it. End of story. Suck it up. No one else cares.

MUTT RULE:
DON'T ASK, DON'T TELL. DON'T CARE.

Who in the hell thought of this genius "Don't Ask, Don't Tell" policy? I mean seriously, God must be rolling around in heaven saying, "damn, I've wasted my best material on these stupid humans." Dogs don't ask because we DON'T CARE. What the hell difference does it matter who you sleep with when you're not in the heat of combat?

CHAPTER TEN

THE PUBLIC EDUCATION SYSTEM:

ABANDON SHIP OR OUTSOURCE OUR FUTURE

Are we all finally ready to admit that your inner city schools are a pipeline for another fine public system, the prison system? I'm just saying, when you need to install metal detectors inside of the school buildings, things just might have gotten a bit out of control.

As a dog, I'm really supportive of reforming your public education. After all, this is our next generation of dog owners. Yeah, that's right, this is strictly for self-preservation, baby. But let's get real for a minute. You people haven't exactly come up with any brilliant ideas to save our future generation yet.

Student incentives? Really. So, let me get this straight. You would pay Missy and Junior to attend school regularly, participate in class, and earn passing grades? Are you friggin' kidding me? In that case, I demand you begin paying me, your loyal companion and trusted protector, for every time I bark, eat my food, and crap only when and where you tell me. Deal? Now do you realize how stupid it sounds to pay someone to do what they should be expected to do for free? Yeah, that's what I thought! As soon as it comes down to investing in your trusty companion, all of a sudden you regain your common sense. But before you slip back into your old patterns, let me help you out.

That's right, man's best friend is going to save the day! I have the answer to strengthen your public school system. Hold on, you need to sit down for this one.

Since the Republicans are always claiming that the way to save any federal problem is to let the private sector run things, now we'll get a chance to see if this strategy could actually work. First, we would ask the lobbyists and private sector to "buy" or "sponsor" (for you sensitive liberals) an inner-city or rural school district. Now, since you Republicans have fled the urban areas to get a better life in the suburbs, we won't need to include those areas in this new overhaul plan.

Using this new funding pool, the "sponsors" would quickly institute a plan to upgrade the infrastructure with state-of-the-art equipment and teaching materials. They could even set up bill boards in the classrooms that could run commercials throughout the building to promote their products. This would have to be done with subliminal messaging of course, under the guise of connecting students to the global community, to keep those annoying civil liberty whiners quiet. Those companies with a lot of passion (cold hard cash, people) for education could even bid to win the honor of renaming the schools, just like you guys do with the sports stadiums. The highest bidder would get their logo and name on the school buildings, uniforms, and honestly everywhere they wanted, if the price was right. Remember people, this is capitalism as its best and this time for a really worthy cause…our future generation!

Wouldn't you feel proud about your little princess attending Google High or Delta Elementary School? Talk about grooming your future workforce and doing something meaningful to prevent your jobs from going overseas.

So, now onto the teachers and those damn unions. I'm so sick and tired of all of you people whining about how little your teachers are paid but every time someone creates a bill to raise taxes to pay your supposedly beloved teachers more money, you vote it down without blinking an eye. So this is where the politicians can really make a difference. This is where I go old school and pull a Robin Hood move. That's right, take from the rich federal politician's salary cuts to give teachers a salary increase! Hey, it's all in the family. We take money from one group of public servants to give it to another group of hard working civil servants. Genius right?

Now this last piece of the puzzle may be a little hard to take for some of you, but stay with me. We propose that you parents actually participate in educating your kids! That's right. Parents would be expected to do homework with your kids and if you need help, then online tutoring will be provided to you. Oh, if your little darling disrupts the class then we will post a streaming video on the dedicated YouTube channel for the public to see what a little delinquent you are raising. Pull it together people and get off of your Facebook and Twitter accounts long enough to realize that your sweet innocent kid can't even string together a coherent written sentence that doesn't require spell check to decode their text-laden shorthand!

What, you say this is too demanding? What the hell are you people smoking these days? Have you seen what the kids in Asia are doing by the time they are in the fifth grade? That's right, they are already speaking two or three languages, designing new mobile apps that you mindless people are buying, and in their spare time, they are training to be in the Olympics. All the while, your little free-spirited kid has learned how to text while watching TV and playing a video game. Wow, how's our future generation looking to you now?

We must work together to save our future dog owners who will be destined to fight for minimum-wage jobs at your local retail shop while they live in your basement because they can't make enough money to get their own place. Are you with me now? Yeah, I thought this would get your attention.

MAX'S TRAINING TIPS
for HUMANS

TIP #1 *You people need to restore* corporal punishment in the classroom! I think a kid would think twice about acting out in school if they knew the teacher could pimp slap them if they got out of line.

TIP #2 I think we should keep the "no child left behind" policy but we really need to consider drop kicking some teachers off the bus! I mean seriously, we need a new litmus test to screen *out* the bad teachers. If you can't pass the state high school graduation exams then, see ya, you're outta here! I mean, if the sound of a kid's voice makes you want to scream, then maybe this isn't the right profession for you. If you believe that berating a child into tears is the best way to get control of a classroom, you may want to explore other careers. If you spend recess running a betting pool on which kids are destined to become convicts, strippers, pimps, or priests, then you definitely need to find another career path.

🐾 MUTT RULE:
STOP the LIES and ACCEPT your FATE

It all starts with that innocent little question: "What do you want to be when you grow up?" The little kid thinks about the answer, as everyone patiently waits for the little genius, who still hasn't mastered his ABCs but can surprisingly sing all the lyrics to "Smack That Ho" without stuttering, to share his dreams. Finally, the kid opens his mouth and says real loud with a smile on his face, "I want to be president when I grow up." Wow, I can't believe the look on the parents and other relatives' faces as they smile with pride and say, "Yes, you can grow up to be president. You'd make a great president!" What the hell are these people thinking?

Okay, I get that we're all supposed to beam with pride when the kid finally learns to use the toilet when he needs to go to the bathroom but dammit, that miracle takes about two to three years for them to learn. Seriously! You only give us dogs two to three months to master this same feat and no one tells us: "Wow, we're so proud of you for not crapping all over our house. You can be the next TV star with your own show."

Face the facts, your little pride and joy peaked at three years old and it's all downhill from there. There's no White House in his future unless he can mow lawns, clean floors, or cook. That's it, people. Find another dream and stop lying to your kids.

SELF-ESTEEM

MOXIE • ROSEVILLE, CA

CHAPTER ELEVEN

WITH AGE COMES WISDOM... OR MAYBE NOT

Ah, to age with grace is everyone's mission except recently you damn humans who are trying to use your supposed intelligence to outsmart the laws of time. When you get older, your stuff is going to sag, most parts of your body will ache, you won't remember things, you won't make as much money, and people will start thinking you're kind of worthless. It amazes us dogs how some of you people will spend *a lot* of money on plastic surgery, Botox, and mid-life crisis toys to make you feel young again. You know who I mean—the celebrities, upper and middle-income people, and those who claim to be younger than their actual age.

Hello, do you think no one is paying attention to how stupid you look? No one—I mean absolutely no one—believes you look ten to twenty years younger than your actual age, you vain fool. In the name of all that's holy, STOP! No wait, keep it up. We dogs are really getting a kick out of this crap. You should hear how we laugh at your latest attempts to defy aging. Oh, not to mention all of the comedians who make successful careers laughing at you. Oh yeah, man, this is good stuff.

What we don't find so funny is how in the hell you let your grown-ass kids come BACK home because they fall on hard times. What the hell is that about? To make matters worse, some of you old geezers are even raising your grown sorry-ass kid's children. Are you friggin' kidding me? Well, I guess since you've obviously done such a great job with your first litter, why not take on another litter? I'm sure this bunch will do much better. Whatever!

Hey, maybe some of these future productive tax-paying citizens will even let you live with them when they grow up and you need their help in your "golden years." Oh, and I bet their place will look familiar to you because it will be YOUR home, stupid. Except now the kids you once worked your butts off to raise will make you move downstairs or in the garage because you won't need much room to slowly die.

MAX'S TRAINING TIPS
for HUMANS

TIP #1   Instead of paying for plastic surgery, Botox, or any other age-defying crap, let's use some of that money to pay for a personal trainer to get your lazy butt in shape. Then get a makeover to dress the best you can for your *actual age*. That's right. Embrace the age on your original birth certificate. When people point out you're getting old, look them straight in the eye and tell them to kiss your old, wrinkled ass.

Remember, the great thing about being old is you get to say whatever you want because people already think you're grumpy so just go with it and give them what they expect. The tip here is to stop caring! Since your memory's shot, live it up. Act like you don't remember the idiots who insult you and when they try to make you remember them, just pee on their leg, smile like it was an accident, and walk away. Thank God you forgot to wear your Depends that day.

TIP #2   Quick, go and burn your bucket list immediately! You know, that list of things you wanted to do before you die but by now, you can't even physically do most things on the damn list anyway. And the other things on the list that you can still manage to do now seem overwhelming. You now realize that you have wasted your really healthy years saying, "I'll get to it next year," only to suddenly realize that you are quickly running out of "next years." This will inevitably send your butt into MORE therapy, which will take even more time away from accomplishing the STUPID LIST!

So, here's the tip, genius: Beginning today, live like tomorrow you'll be taken for a ride to the vet, with no advanced warning, for an unscheduled visit with the weird guy in the white lab coat. Live like tomorrow's going to be the end. Get it?

TIP #3 When your little pride and joy calls to ask or tell you that they need to move back home, grow a set of balls the size of a pit bull (trust me, these dog's balls are huge) and tell junior there's no way in hell that's going to happen. Then quickly hang up the phone without saying another word.

Tell your spouse the new rule. That's right, RULE! Remember in your pack there's only room for one alpha lead. If they don't agree then they can get the hell out and live with their kid, who is soon to be homeless because they don't know how to work two to three jobs while they trim their expenses.

TIP #4 When your same soon-to-be homeless child asks if you can take care of your grandkids for a little bit until they get back on their feet, you apply the guidance in **training tip #3**…NO! There's one more thing you will need to do now that you have put your foot down—change the house locks. It will cost you, but in the end, this will save you from those little bastards breaking into your home with your spare key under the guise of wanting to "check up on you."

Plan to use online video chat for a while, just so that you can keep in touch with your grandkids. You don't want to run the risk of your kids pulling a fast one on you at the end of a family gathering with the old, "hey, can you keep an eye on the kids while we load the car?" Sounds innocent enough, but it's just a set-up for an eat-n-run. Also, absolutely no babysitting, even if it's at their home. This is just another bait and switch tactic. Basically, there will be no in-person contact until you audit their financial records to confirm that they are back on their feet. Believe me, this will all be money and time well spent. This is all about preserving YOUR retirement fund!

MUTT RULE:
STOP BUYING SELF-HELP BOOKS if YOU don't APPLY the ADVICE

This one is strictly for you WOMEN. Are you listening to me? Ok good. Here it is, the straight truth. The best relationship advice you'll ever get. If you don't have a solid, loving relationship by your mid-40s and you've been trying, then you need to change your game plan.

Here is the raw truth to the questions you've been asking for years: No, it's not stupid to stroke a man's ego. Yes, you should get a professional makeover and dress to flatter your current shape, not the one you hope to have one day. No, all of the good men aren't gone. Yes, your standards are too unrealistic if you don't possess most of the same qualities that are on your "man checklist." No, it's not considered giving up when you go on dates just to get out and have fun. Yes, you can be direct without being nasty. And no, you shouldn't complain about the type of men you meet online if you keep posting half-naked pictures of yourself straddled across the bed.

Finally, the most important tip, if you CAN'T keep your dog interested in listening to you for at least ten consecutive minutes without them falling asleep, turning their back to you, or worse yet, walking away, then yes, you need to work on your conversation skills.

If this hits a nerve with you then go ahead and buy ten cats, get fat, and embrace your future alone because you won't get a man or a dog. Enjoy!

Save your money and stop buying self-help books that you clearly aren't applying to your life. Here's a new idea, just buy one book and actually do what it suggests!

CHAPTER TWELVE

SAY IT LOUD, I'M UGLY AND I'M PROUD!

Here's another area where we really don't get you people...low self-esteem and self-confidence. What the hell is wrong with you guys? Are you people smoking crack, all day, every day? Damn. I mean take a look at your local dog shelter some time. Not exactly the best of the litter, but we make the most of our situation. We don't need to pay a therapist to help us examine our childhood to find someone to blame for our inability to deal with the fact that we may look like a hyena (damn, they are part of the canine tree but they have a face only a mother can love). Nor do we spend hundreds of dollars on clothes and makeup to try to overcompensate for the truth. That's right, we all can't be show dogs.

Look in the mirror and embrace your reality like dogs do every day. Say it with me: "Hi, my name is ____ and I'm ugly!"

Dogs are fully aware of our looks but it doesn't matter. Have you ever noticed that no matter how a dog looks, they do the same thing—they strut down the street, head held high, and tail wagging. That's right, we walk like our shit doesn't stink!

Don't laugh! Remember, we manipulated you people to holding an *annual* ugliest dog in the world contest, which you happily televise. You even offer us some great prizes, magazine covers, product endorsements, and interviews glorifying the very thing that you people are trying to work out in therapy—your looks.

MAX'S TRAINING TIPS
for HUMANS

TIP #1 Hold an anti-beauty pageant—the ugliest woman and man in the world contest. I bet you could get some cable channel to host this train wreck, I mean… pageant. I know you won't have any shortage of potential contestants either. Given your fascination with being a celebrity at any cost, I'm sure you'll have many aspiring uglies standing in line for hours desperately vying for the chance to compete for the honor of being named "the ugliest woman or man in the world."

TIP #2 Since the root of much of your self-esteem issues seems to be your fathers, I have a novel tip. Go find your sperm donor, I mean your father, at a family reunion or cookout. It's a perfect setting for an ambush, which is what you're going to do here.

After a nice smile and some chit-chat to relax him, quickly unleash all of your years of pent-up anger, drunken mistakes, lost opportunities, and basically the pathetic situation that is your life. Then tell him what a miserable excuse of a human being he is. Next, give him his last father's day gift, EVER, pee on his leg, and walk away!

Now I have to warn you that your "father of the year" nominee won't tolerate this crazy public outburst from his child for more than a few minutes, so you'll need to speak fast and be prepared to duck after dear old dad realizes what you're saying. You also won't be invited to any other family gatherings because even though your dad might be the idiot you claimed he was in your therapy sessions, no one else cares.

Also, here's a newsflash, the apple doesn't fall far from the tree so it's no surprise everyone thinks you're a jackass who's destined to be blamed for everything in your sperm recipient's life too! Isn't karma wonderful?

TIP #2 *Embrace your character flaws.* That's right, wear them like a badge on a boy scout's banner. Since you people like attention and awards for EVERYTHING, even if you don't deserve it, let's create a series of badges for every stupid little condition that you claim is to blame for your flaws.

Obese because the food industry has forced you to overeat and become fat? Yep, we got a badge for your big behind.

Unattractive because your parents couldn't find someone more attractive to con into having a baby? Yep, we got a badge of honor for that one too.

Not quite a Rhodes Scholar because maybe your parents were very close relatives but they thought it was okay to love one another, just one time? Oh yeah, we even have a badge for you people, too. Although I don't think many of you will wear this last badge because let's be honest, those who need to wear this badge are too dumb to realize it.

MUTT RULE:
EVERYONE CAN'T be a WINNER

You know, I really hate reality TV but there are two shows that hit the nail on the head...the *Biggest Loser* and *The Apprentice*. Those shows got it right. Not everyone can be a winner. What the hell is it with you people always expecting an award for just showing up? Come on, this has gotten ridiculous. There's nothing wrong with being a loser, it used to build character but oh wait, that doesn't play well on TV anymore does it?

CHAPTER THIRTEEN

THERE'S HONOR IN BEING A LOSER

Oh my God! I can't believe I won the BLUE RIBBON for the best looking mutt under 10 years old who was rescued from a kennel that now lives in my town contest! I'll never forget the look on my owner's face as they put that beautiful shiny ribbon on my dog collar. That was a real moment of pride until I looked around and realized that every other dog, even the damn poodle shepherd mix, had the same ribbon. But my owner said I won and that I was the best dog in the contest. I was robbed! Since when did the "winner" have to share the same prize with the losers? And, why the hell can't we acknowledge everybody else as "losers"? After all, we don't invite all of the presidential candidates to sit on the stage for the inauguration ceremony. Imagine what that would be like.

One by one, invite them to the podium to recite their "honorary" acceptance speech for NOT becoming president. No, instead we make them sit at home bitterly watching the ceremony while drinking shots of vodka every time the newly elected president, who is now referred to as "that idiot," says how he's humbled by their victory or promises to keep their campaign promises. Yes, that's the taste of victory...sweet if you win but bitter if you lose.

There's nothing wrong with losing and the sooner you humans embrace the badge of being a loser, the better off everyone will become. I mean, aren't you tired of listening to people rationalize why they lost? Or worse yet, aren't you tired of having to give that faux support to the losers in your life when all you really want to say is "You suck! That's why you didn't win. Get over it and move on. The other guy really did deserve to win, and it wasn't even a close race. I mean, you lost by a LOT." Wow, doesn't that sound better to say? I know it will be hard at first, so let's start by practicing on your kids.

Really, it's okay and you know damn well that little Johnny and Shanequa had better get used to hearing "No, I'm sorry we've given the job to someone more qualified who we could actually understand without referring to the dictionary for dumbasses." So here's what you say when the little one comes home crying because he didn't make the baseball team. Using your newfound spine, look the teary eyed kid straight in the face and get real close so he hear every word of your loving support and tell him: "I'm sorry that you didn't make the team but I saw you practice and you were AWFUL. The other kids were better than you."

Now I know this next part may seem rough but trust me, this is for their own good. They'll thank you in about twenty years after they get out of rehab, do a short stint in jail, and spend time in therapy. But for now, they will hate your guts.

To soften things a little bit, use one of these sorry lines that your parents used on you. Acknowledge that this maybe painful to hear and it hurts you more to say it (ok, this is a lie but necessary to stop junior from totally losing it and killing you in your sleep) but it's time they found a new dream, one they can actually stand a chance at doing and getting paid for so that YOU won't have to spend your golden years supporting the little loser.

I mean seriously, it's really sad to see a kid waste their youth chasing a dream, getting "faux awards" that they really didn't deserve, all because you damn adults were "afraid" to break their little hearts and NOT give them a prize for losing. Are you all that hell bent on raising another generation of out of touch, *Jersey Shore* loving losers who earn a living for getting drunk, cursing, fighting on cue, and basically acting like an ass in the hopes of getting a reality show and then possibly hitting it big time with a spread in *Pimps and Hoes*?

If that thought scares the hell out of you, and it should, then get cracking with the real, no-holds-barred truth and save that bull for your spouse.

MAX'S TRAINING TIPS
for HUMANS

TIP #1 Establish rules as to what it means to honestly EARN an award, as opposed to being given a "faux award." A "real award" is anything that you were given for an accomplishment, where you worked hard to win, and this is the critical component here, someone else was openly acknowledged as the LOSER. Also, to validate a "real award" you will need to have a comparison of all of the awards given for this accomplishment so that we can note the disparity between each of the so-called award recipients. The bigger the disparity in the awards between first place and the other awardees, the more valid the "real award" will be. Now, if you can get a picture of the award ceremony with the "losers" crying or holding their head in shame, then that would be an added bonus.

TIP #2 Take all of the underserved trophies, which will now be referred to as "faux awards" and remove them from your home right now! That's right, take every "faux award" that you know damn well was either a pity award or an award for just showing up and toss them into a box. As a matter of fact, get the whole family in on the act and make everyone put their "faux awards" into the box. They'll probably cry but tell them to suck it up. This is the first step towards REALITY, people! From now on, the only awards that anyone will be allowed to even bring into your home will be "real awards" that are truly EARNED!

MUTT RULE:
MIND your OWN DAMN BUSINESS!

Not all, but many of you humans have this uncontrollable urge to publicly offer your opinions or just random comments on situations that don't involve you, at all. This isn't Facebook where everybody gets a chance to chime in on everything; this is the real world where you can get beat down for running your mouth to complete strangers.

This problem appears to get worse as you get older, too. I'll never forget the day my owner's mom came for a visit. That old heifer had the nerve to tell my owner "That dog is so misbehaved. Really, he's spoiled rotten." My owner defended me, as she should, but that lady kept right on nagging, saying, "Why don't you make him sit on the floor instead of the chair? He's not human, he's just a dog!" *Oh no she didn't!* I almost lunged at her but I knew my owner would have shipped me off to the shelter.

Focus on fixing your own jacked up relationships and lazy wayward kids first, then you can help somebody else out. There's only one OPRAH AND IT AIN'T you. Guess what? No one else cares what you think! You may get away with that crap at work and home but aside from those places, we're gonna need you to keep your opinions to yourselves.

CHAPTER FOURTEEN

FORGET THE WEEKEND WARRIOR, EMBRACE YOUR INNER COUCH POTATO

Just like you people, we dogs live for the weekends! There's nothing better than spending time with our beloved owners going for a run, hike, or just trying out some new intense workout to help you people get back in shape. What a joke! When will you folks realize that you're not young anymore? Seriously, you just can't spend five days stuffing your face watching TV, while you text and post lame Facebook updates about how great your life is, then suddenly it's Saturday morning and we are forced to watch you squeeze your behind into workout clothes to attempt to "go all out" like you thought you did when you were younger. Newsflash, not only do you people look stupid wearing clothes that don't fit, but time has not been kind to you. You can't do extreme sports now and to be honest with you, you really weren't that athletic when you were younger either.

I'm going to schedule an intervention for you. You need to see how your weekend antics are starting to jeopardize the quality of our lives and breaking apart our families. That's right, I'm embarrassed to watch the neighbors laugh at you behind your back when you leave the house in your workout gear that's too tight. You even have the nerve to buy the top brand equipment, protective gear, and those damn energy drinks when everyone knows you'll run out of breath as soon as you break a sweat. You don't need sports drinks, you need to pull up from the table and give up a few of those second helpings that you have every night.

I'm not alone with my disgust. That's right, your family and I have talked and we all feel the same way! I actually saw the look of utter shame and disgust on Junior's face when you volunteered not once but three times to coach his softball team. Hello, didn't you get the hint the first few times when everyone politely told you that they didn't want to interfere with your busy work schedule? To everyone's surprise and relief the guy in the wheelchair rolled over to say that he had time to coach, even though he never played before. Remember how all of the parents quickly voted for the wheelchair guy as the new coach and relegated you to bring the drinks?

Our economy is depending on you overweight people to maintain your lifestyle and purchase those pills, you know, the ones that you claim are your right to have and no damn government is going to tell you what to do with your body. Just put away your new workout clothes, get back on the couch, and I'll fetch your orthopedic sneakers when you're ready to take me for my stroll. No wait, I'll have Junior take me out for my walk, after all he needs to start earning his keep around this house!

See, everybody wins so just relax and rub your belly as you channel surf.

MAX'S TRAINING TIPS
for HUMANS

TIP #1   Don't let those stupid infomercials convince you that you will turn your lumpy, bloated ass into a lean temple that will be the envy of all of your friends. It's a big lie! It will never happen! I can tell you for a fact after watching you nearly die trying to copy those extreme exercise moves from the comfort of your couch that you are destined to be fat and a burden to society for a long time. After all, this is why you pay for that expensive insurance policy that you don't want the poor people to get.

There are nice pills available to help extend your life so that you can continue to enjoy your current lifestyle without the interruption of exercise. Say it with me, "exercise infomercials are not my friend."

TIP #2   Since these days nearly all of your friends are virtual anyway, why are you falling prey to peer pressure about getting in shape? As long as someone in this damn house can walk and feed me then I say, forget them! I mean, your kids know CPR and ever since you bought that portable defibrillator on the internet, you don't have anything to worry about when you pass out the next time you try to bend over while trying to tie your sneakers. Now, we should probably lose the sneakers with the laces and switch to the slip on sneakers. That's right, the time has come to accept the fact that you have become your parents. So just squeeze your big feet into those nice cushioned geriatric slippers and shuffle on over to the refrigerator for the snack before the commercial break ends.

MUTT RULE:
DOG OWNERSHIP is the SECRET to GOOD HEALTH

Dogs are so concerned about our owner's health that we're going to take matters into our own paws. Dogs have formed a new group, Mutts United, to commit to whip you people into shape. Get ready, folks, we have hired a top-notch public relations firm, you know, one of those fancy Hollywood firms that promotes those no-talent reality stars. Yeah, that's right, we mean business and we have the data to back it up.

Mutts United surveyed adults and found that, on average, dog owners live healthier, happier, and longer lives. They also have three times more sex and earn twice the annual salary of non-dog owners. Oh yeah, before you ask, all other pet owners, especially those with cats generally live shorter, boring, and hermit-like lives. We didn't get a chance to ask them about their sex lives because frankly, we couldn't understand them through their crying. If you need more proof than this that dogs can improve your life, then you don't deserve a dog! Put this book down now, go buy a cat, and forget everything that you've read.

STEREOTYPES ARE REAL PEOPLE

This political correctness mess is such a load of crap! I mean seriously, why do you people get so offended by this whole stereotyping stuff anyway? Look around, people; stereotypes are based on reality. Seriously! I mean black people are too quick to pull the race card, laugh too loud, and yes, they do like fried chicken. White folks do assume everyone knows the lyrics to the latest pop song, do buy most of the gangsta rap CDs, and are quick to speak "black" to try to show how cool they are to their black friend/co-worker/complete stranger. Hispanics do know someone who's an illegal immigrant, like to travel in groups, eat a lot of beans, and act like they can't speak English when it's convenient. Hello, we never said that stereotypes apply to EVERYONE, but most of you can find at least one thing that applies to your uptight behind! So can't we all just get along? Lighten up and just laugh at how stupid we've gotten trying to label everybody else into some group, just so that we can understand how they operate.

It's really simple—if you don't like stereotypes then stop doing things to perpetuate them! Really, it's not that difficult to do. Hmm, let's think about it for a minute before you jump up to protest this book. C'mon, you people are all for freedom of speech right up until someone begins to speak the truth. I maybe a dog, but dammit, I speak for all of your pets when I say, "get over yourself"!

MAX'S TRAINING TIPS
for HUMANS

TIP #1 I only have one tip for this area of your life because, as I have said before, you people are tiring me out with all of your soft, spineless, whiny complaints. So here's the tip, just embrace your stereotype. That's it!

So let's say the next time you black people are hanging out with your white friends and they ask you to tell them what the black people think about the latest professional athlete who got arrested for some stupid crime, stop and follow my tip. Since most people think that black people are too sensitive about "being wronged by the man" just react like they expect you to. That's right, roll your eyes, cuss them out real loud, and remind them that you don't speak for all black people, dammit! Then throw their drink in their face. After all, you don't want to waste your own perfectly good drink.

Then, the next day apologize to your boss and offer to work late to help them out with that big presentation. Your white boss will also embrace their stereotype, as they smile and accept your apology. Just as soon as you turn around, security will be behind you to escort your black butt out of the building. "You're fired!" your still smiling white boss will say, because true to their stereotype, white people will smile as they cut you. I'm just saying, that's the word in the dog park.

 **MUTT RULE:**

There are no rules for this topic because I don't think you people can let go of your political correctness long enough to get my wisdom. So, no mutt rule for you!

PARENTING

JAZ • AUSTIN, TX

CHAPTER SIXTEEN

PEARLS OF WISDOM OR CUBIC ZIRCONIUM CRAP?

STOP LYING TO YOUR KIDS

Ah I'll never forget growing up with my owner's kids. Those early years were great! I especially loved listening to all of the wisdom and bedtime stories that you shared with your young kids. I know you parents mean well but I gotta tell you that some of those so-called pearls of wisdom and wholesome fables were a load of crap! You really need to stop. Why do you believe that you need to protect little Johnny and Susie from the reality of life by telling them lies and old wives tales?

Like the one about finishing all of the food on their plates so that they can grow up to be big and strong. Oh yeah, they'll grow up to be big alright, big as a house! Have you looked around a park lately and noticed all of the overweight kids? And before you say it, they all can't have "a gland problem." I'm just saying,

I don't think it would hurt a lot of these kids if they left some food on the plate every once in a while.

Let's not forget the nice little tale about old Mother Hubbard who went to the cupboard to get her poor dog a bone. But when she got there the cupboard was bare and then her poor dog had none. What kind of ghetto mess is this; some poor single lady who was too broke to feed her sweet loyal dog, who by the way was probably forced to listen to her constant complaining about her sad life, all while on an empty stomach. This isn't a fairy tale that would comfort your children before they go to bed unless you're intentionally trying to have them wake up in the middle of the night screaming because they had nightmares that they grew up to be broke, living in a shack with a mangy dog named Scruffy.

Let's stop dressing these stories up as just a sweet innocent part of childhood. They're not cute or innocent. They're huge friggin' lies! The sooner your kids embrace reality, the sooner we can get them off Prozac and get them back to learning so they can make money to pay for your retirement home because those little ingrates are sure as hell not going to let you live with them and their third spouse. How's that for a pearl of wisdom?

MAX'S TRAINING TIPS
for HUMANS

TIP #1 When you tuck your little bundle of joy in to bed, instead of reading them a fairy tale let's review your financial portfolio with them. That's right. If you want to tell them a feel good story to inspire them, just share the highs and lows of their dad's acclaimed stock picking abilities. After all, in a few short years, they're going to be embarrassed and disappointed by everything you do as parents anyway so why not just speed things up and let them face reality at an earlier age?

This game plan should put the kids in therapy sooner but on the bright side, they can work out all of their angst on the playground. Or would you rather they just wait until they become teenagers and they date some no-good delinquent just to get back at you?

TIP #2 Since you people are eager to get your kids into every program imaginable, you know, to give them a better life than you had and prove to your annoying cousin Chuck that your kids are smarter than his, here's yet another reason to skip the fairy tales. Start reading the classics to your kids...Shakespeare, Tolstoy, Hemingway. Ah yes, the great stories that your behind barely remembers reading when you partied your way through college. Remember those hazy years?

Now is your chance to build a legacy that you can be proud of, one that's worthy of your years of sacrifice. If that seems too heavy for you, then just go ahead and pick out your kid's stage name and start having them practice their pole dancing routine.

🐾 MUTT RULE:
TIMEOUTS are BANNED

People, when will you learn to stop this damn weasel approach to disciplining your kids? The only way to get these kids attention is with a belt! That's right. I said it! You remember that thing your dad used to keep your little behinds in line before the liberal softies told you "its inhumane to beat your kids. You'll scar them for life. Talk to them, don't hit them." When the hell do you ever just talk to your dog when the poor thing falls out of your good graces? That's right, NEVER.

Come on, toughen up, and take off your belt like your parents, grandparents, and all of your forefathers have done for centuries before you, and whip some tail first, then talk later. If I told you people that your founding fathers said it was okay, then all of sudden I bet you would see the wisdom of my rule.

CHAPTER SEVENTEEN

SWEET SIXTEEN BIRTHDAY BASH, NEXT STOP REHAB

Okay, maybe we dogs aren't the best example of parenting since we don't get to raise our puppies, thanks to you owners who refuse to keep our litter to make room for your precious little kids. Anyway, I may be wrong but if my puppy cussed me out and acted like a fool in the playground in front of my playgroup I would grab them by their neck, pin them down on the ground, and beat their butt in front of everyone. But somehow you people think your little precious angel, who can hardly stand spending time with you, let alone show you respect as a parent should get a huge birthday celebration for turning "sweet sixteen." Are you kidding me? Is this the same kid who we watched throw a fit because you wouldn't buy her an iPhone? Now, somehow Princess deserves a brand new car and a birthday party at a nightclub with over 100 of her closest ungrateful friends? Really, what did I miss?

Maybe instead of "sweet sixteen" they should call it "selfish sixteen"! I mean seriously, I've watched reality TV with you people and these damn kids have lost their minds.

MAX'S TRAINING TIPS
for HUMANS

TIP #1 When your little angel finishes telling you what she wants for her milestone sixteenth birthday, just lean back in your chair, smile, and open a box filled with the "wonderful" birthday gifts that you've received over the years from your "thoughtful" child. Oh yeah, as soon as they realize what you have in the box, this little stroll down memory lane will start to get uncomfortable real fast for the kid, but don't let that stop you.

As you pull out one after another of the cheap, thoughtless ties, cheesy mugs, and trifling handmade cards, your emotions and the expression on her face should make things really uncomfortable for the little angel. This is the perfect time to announce what your gift to her will be. Look your pride and joy directly in her pretty little face and say without blinking an eye: "You can continue living in MY home for two more years, rent free. Tada, what do you think?" Oh yeah, don't forget to throw some confetti as you yell, "happy birthday"!

TIP #2 If you have more than one kid you'll need to make an example out of the oldest one's milestone birthday or the younger ones will blackmail you, oops, I mean point out the disparity in their birthday celebrations. If you go all out for the first one, then damnit, you gotta keep this crap up for all of your other kids, so both parents are going to need to stick together on this one.

The goal here is to set the bar really low so they all know not to expect any big party or major gift on their sixteenth birthday...period! If the kids whine about how unfair that is, then give them a choice. They can either have a blowout birthday party with their college fund that you sacrificed to create, or they can save this money to pay for their four-year college degree. It's their choice. Either way, since you've been borrowing from this account for the last few years to splurge on things like the mortgage and clothes, it will either be a ghetto fabulous party or a few night classes at the local community college. So live it up!

MUTT RULE:
RETRAIN YOURSELF to RECLAIM your HOME

Okay, now this Dog Whisperer, Cesar Milan, is brilliant. He's convinced you humans to think that he's training dogs to behave, when he is actually re-training humans to stand their ground and take charge of their homes. This is pure genius! Watch and learn, people.

At the beginning of the so-called training session, these distraught grown adults tell a sob story about how they need help with their uncontrollable, bad dog. It's no surprise that many of these people are also the ones you see in the supermarket as their children run wild down the aisles, bumping into people, and rolling on the floor screaming, "buy me a f...ing candy bar right now!" But for some strange reason, these people can't understand why they can't make their dogs behave.

Hello, dogs are going to do the same wild-ass behavior that we see your little pride and joy get away with every day.

The real re-training begins when the Dog Whisperer enters the home. He glides into the room oozing with confidence and a swagger that any rapper would envy, like the leader of the pack...any pack. He quietly commands respect with a look and few words unlike you people who yell at the top of your lungs while everyone ignores you. He never raises his voice because within a matter of minutes, everyone knows who's running the show. When a dog tries to get out of line, Cesar quickly gets in their face, tightens the leash, says a few short words, and bam, order is restored. Now that's how you should run your home, people! Straighten up, grow some balls, and run your home like the Dog Whisperer.

CHAPTER EIGHTEEN

DISEASE DU JOUR

Why is it that everywhere you turn these days diseases that were once rarely mentioned now seem to be so common place? Do most adults now really have ADD or are people just fed up with listening to one another's trivial crap? Are your children struggling to overcome dyslexia or are the little darlings just too lazy to read anything that's not written in text shorthand, and in less than 140 characters?

Almost every week there's a new study out that supports your excuse for bad behavior. Do you find yourself yelling at other drivers on the highway and cussing out elderly drivers at stop lights? No problem, one diagnosis of PMS coming right up. What, you say you can't seem to lose those stubborn excess fifty pounds? No worries my friend, it's not your fault, it's just a thyroid disorder that your parents gave you. Yep, bad genes!

You wanted to cuss out your co-worker and knew you would get fired for saying what's on your mind, so think quick. Yeah, "I have Tourettes Syndrome and the medication makes me loopy so I'm just trying to work through it naturally." Naturally, my behind.

Free yourselves from these lies people and just admit the truth! You have LAZY UNDERACHIEVER SYNDROME mixed with a slight bout of "I hate peoplitis"!

MAX'S TRAINING TIPS
for HUMANS

TIP #1   **Starting today,** you should all just throw away any of your medications that mask your true emotions. That's right, down the drain with the drugs that "even out" your personality. It's time to unleash your true personality and let the world love it or leave it, baby! You need to strip down and get buck naked with your emotions! Let the breeze blow as you walk around buck naked and drug free!

TIP #2   **If you followed the first tip fully,** you've probably been committed to a nice "retreat center" where you can "work things out" away from the hassles of your daily life. Perfect! Now you can get away from your job and family for awhile without any guilt! Of course, when you get released everyone will talk in real soft tones when they speak to you because they are concerned that you'll relapse or worse yet, freak out and stab them. Either way, it's good to keep them guessing. Fear is a good protector.

MUTT RULE:
DOMESTIC KIDS ROCK

Okay, as a mutt, I really understand the interest in adopting kids of different cultures from your own. Pedigrees are so over-rated anyway. But what I can't figure out is why in the hell you feel that you have to go overseas to adopt a foreign child when little Chiquita and Jabarri need homes, too, and they live right down the street from you.

Sure, they don't have that exotic look that says, "Hey, look at me I'm a big-hearted liberal who makes a lot money so I don't have to adopt a domestic kid, I can get an imported baby." But seriously, do you need to fly half way around the world to boost your image?

If you want exotic, we can give these domestic kids a makeover for you. We will hire a celebrity stylist to start dressing the kids in the latest "refugee meets urban chic" look. These upgraded domestic kids will come complete with a wardrobe in a color scheme to fit right into your new family photos.

Now we've got your attention, don't we? This puts a whole new spin on customization!

CHAPTER NINETEEN

CREATIVE GENIUS OR JUST PLAIN CRAZY?

Why are you people so willing to overlook crazy when it's dressed up as a pop icon? No, crazy is still crazy, even if it just won a Grammy!

If one of your co-workers suddenly jumped up during the middle of a staff meeting, cutting you off during your big presentation, you would tell them to sit down and shut up! Then, everyone would jump on their Twitter and Facebook accounts to report on what your co-worker Bob just did. Some people would be outraged. Others would sympathize with the situation and say, "poor Bob was just misunderstood. He's one of our best employees. After all, he just lost his mother so you know he's still grieving." Seriously, are you going to pull the grief card? No, Bob is a jerk who just happens to be talented and makes a lot of money for the company but that's his only real upside here.

Need another example? Let's just say that one day I can't find my favorite bone, and you know how much that means to a dog.

So, out of frustration, I jump up on your dining room table in the middle of dinner and snatch the steak bone right off your plate. Remember, I'm devastated about my bone and I'm not in my right mind. Would you console me and let me have your bone? Yeah right! I wouldn't get any sympathy from your selfish behind. No sooner had you snatched that steak bone out of my mouth then I would have been rushed to the car and found myself being dropped off at the nearest shelter. You probably wouldn't even look back on your way out the door.

So, why are you all so willing to look the other way just because someone has money or fame? If Bob was a hard-working guy who worked at a fast food restaurant and pushed his co-worker, a cute teenage blonde, away from the register while she was in the middle of taking an order, and he started going off about how he really deserved to work the register rather than the grill, he would get smacked down in a second. That's right, smack down first, and ask questions later.

MAX'S TRAINING TIPS
for HUMANS

TIP #1   I'm no expert but I can tell you people what's wrong with your behavior these days. There are too many self-indulgent lunatics running around in the streets! Stop making excuses for these spoiled brats and treat them like everybody else. Make them go to rehab or kick their butts out of your house and shun them until they get their acts together.

TIP #2 Stop covering these deviants and their latest antics in the media! Really, have a media boycott of all coverage of the crazy or drugged-out celebrities until they're out of rehab. You'll be surprised at how fast they'll get clean and back to "normal" once no one in the media wants to cover their every move.

MUTT RULE:
DOG CRATES are the NEW PRIVATE RETREAT for KIDS

Here's a little hint people, if you can't get your little bundle of joy or fruit of your loins to follow your directions without 50 friggin' time-outs, then just put them in one of our dog crates for about 15 minutes. I know this may sound extreme and Child Protective Services will definitely haul your butt in on charges, but at least things will be quiet in your home for a little while.

MAX'S DECREE FOR LIVING UNLEASHED

Since most of you people don't even follow God's 10 Commandments and you don't want to be told what to do, here are Max's parting tips that you may or may not consider reflecting on to improve your life. Follow them if you like, but if not, hey at least you bought my book, so just keep on living your life and pee where you want! That's it!

 ### Thou shalt not crap where you sleep.

It sounds so simple, yet so many of you people screw this up. Never, ever sleep with the babysitter, nanny, cleaning lady, gardener, or pool boy! Unless you're actually trying to publicly humiliate your family.

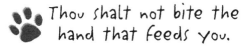
Thou shalt not bite the hand that feeds you.

Although you may be tempted to, trust me on this one, it never works out well.

Thou shalt not follow the pack.

If you need an explanation then re-read the damn book!

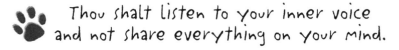 **Thou shalt listen to your inner voice and not share everything on your mind.**

When you're tempted to share one of your "pearls of wisdom" with someone, just hold back. You'll find 90 percent of the time it's not a pearl, it's just gas. Let it pass and keep it moving.

Thou shalt not hold grudges.

Most things won't matter in a few days anyway. Bitterness just makes you miserable, fat, and ugly from replaying the situation in your mind and forcing other people to listen to "did I tell you what that fool did to me?" stories that honestly no one else cares about. LET IT GO!

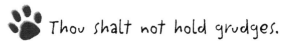 **Thou shalt treat your family like you treat your balls.**

Protect them from all harm, keep them clean at all times, and shower them with a lot of affection. Ladies, let's substitute your equivalent body part for this analogy.

Thou shalt age like a dog.

Squeeze seven years worth of life into every one of your human years. Really make the most out of every minute—rest, play, work, and love like you're off the leash!

 ## Thou shalt never stop chasing squirrels.

Why, you ask? Because it makes us dogs happy and you humans could certainly use more happiness in your lives. Pure and simple, skip the psychological bull. Find the "squirrel" in your life and chase it every day. Be happy going after whatever makes you happy, no matter what everyone else says or what type of strange looks you get. As long as you're happy and no one gets hurt, go for it. I'll let you in on a little secret...we never catch the damn squirrel and it's really not the point. We just like chasing them up trees and around parks, because we CAN.

MAX'S UNLEASHED CREW

MAx • FRANKLIN, TN

OTIS • NASHVILLE, TN
"YOU REALLY WOKE ME UP TO TELL ME THIS?"

IGGY • NASHVILLE, TN
"YEAH, I BIT THE MAIL MAN, BUT HE WAS ASKING FOR IT."

YUKON CORNELIUS • PEGRAM, TN
"I PROMISE, GOD, I DIDN'T DO IT THIS TIME."

ACKNOWLEDGMENTS

To my beloved Max, one of my best friends and the inspiration for this book. I was blessed to have him in my life for nearly 16 wonderful years. I never knew exactly what kind of dog he was, but a few months after rescuing him from a shelter; it didn't seem to matter anymore. He was simply Max, my baby. A proud mutt who stood out in any crowd.

Max understood me like only a few others have in my life. Sometimes the look he would give me, with those big black eyes, would let me know that I was acting crazy and needed to come back to reality. Only dog owners will truly understand what it is like to have such a wonderful companion who never needs words to communicate with you. You were one in a million Max!

To my patient editor, Alice Sullivan, you were truly a godsend. Your honest critique was always delivered in a way that preserved my ego. Thanks for hanging in there with me through my procrastination and fear of publicly sharing my work.

While I was doing my research for this book and trying to find my theme I was blessed to bump into a young boy, Grey, in a bookstore one evening who inspired me to find my voice for *Pee Where You Want*. Grey was wise beyond his years and to this day, I believe he was put into my path to help me write my second attempt at my "first book".

I want to thank my family and friends who encouraged me to write and calmed me down when I doubted my vision. I especially want to thank my brother and sister in-law, Mark Thompson and Jennifer Thompson, who read every chapter and provided their honest feedback. Sometimes too honest, but it was always appreciated. Even when I would send them, what I thought was brilliant writing at two o'clock in the morning they would always find time to respond. They did all of this while raising four kids, including one with special needs who required a great deal of extra attention. I love you guys!

To my wonderful and funny mother, Deana Thompson, who always encouraged me to dream big and trust in God. You are funnier than you realize Mommy. To my uncle, Ben Simmons, who from the time I was a child showed me how to embrace my creativity even when no one else got it. One of his best life lessons was when he showed my brothers and I how to streak in the 70's because he said that it would free us from the conventional crap of society. Okay, he taught us this little lesson when my parents were on vacation but I'll never forget that experience. He shared his feedback on the early drafts of the book and filmed my book trailer. You're almost seventy years old and still amazing!

Thanks to my other family and friends for your support: Dolores Kelly, Jonathan Thompson, Russ Gannon, Jenese Camper, Robin Dunlap, Lisa Bailey, Wayne Procope, Clarence Clark, Chris Mason, Dell Oliver, Sherri Neal, Cheryl Mason, Raye Rose, Christina Coldiron, Paula Williams, Vikki Harriman, Erica Rocheteau Donalson, Bonny Mossey, Dena Fermino.

Finally, to my dad, Roy Thompson, who now guides me from heaven. There is hardly a day that goes by that I don't stop and seek your advice. You were my best friend, confidant, and cheerleader. More than anyone else, this book is for you. You always told me that I had a gift that would one day be shared with many people. I'll always love you Daddy!

ABOUT THE AUTHOR

Inspired by countless talks (often one-sided, of course), Karen Thompson wrote what she believes Max, and all dogs are really thinking about their owners, politics, kids, and life in general. An avid dog lover and mommy to shelter-dog, Max, for nearly 17 years, Karen has gained a unique perspective on pop culture through the eyes of her loyal companion Max. After listening to all of her whining and ranting for 17 years, Max sadly passed away last year. His passing motivated Karen to finally answer the one question that she always asked Max: "What do you think I should do with my life, boy?" After spending the last 25 years grinding away in corporate America, not so quietly spewing out sarcasms about the insanely stupid things she's seen along the way, Karen has decided to take Max's "advice" to pursue her life's passion of writing. *Pee Where You Want* is Karen's first book.

2757431R00060

Printed in Great Britain
by Amazon.co.uk, Ltd.,
Marston Gate.